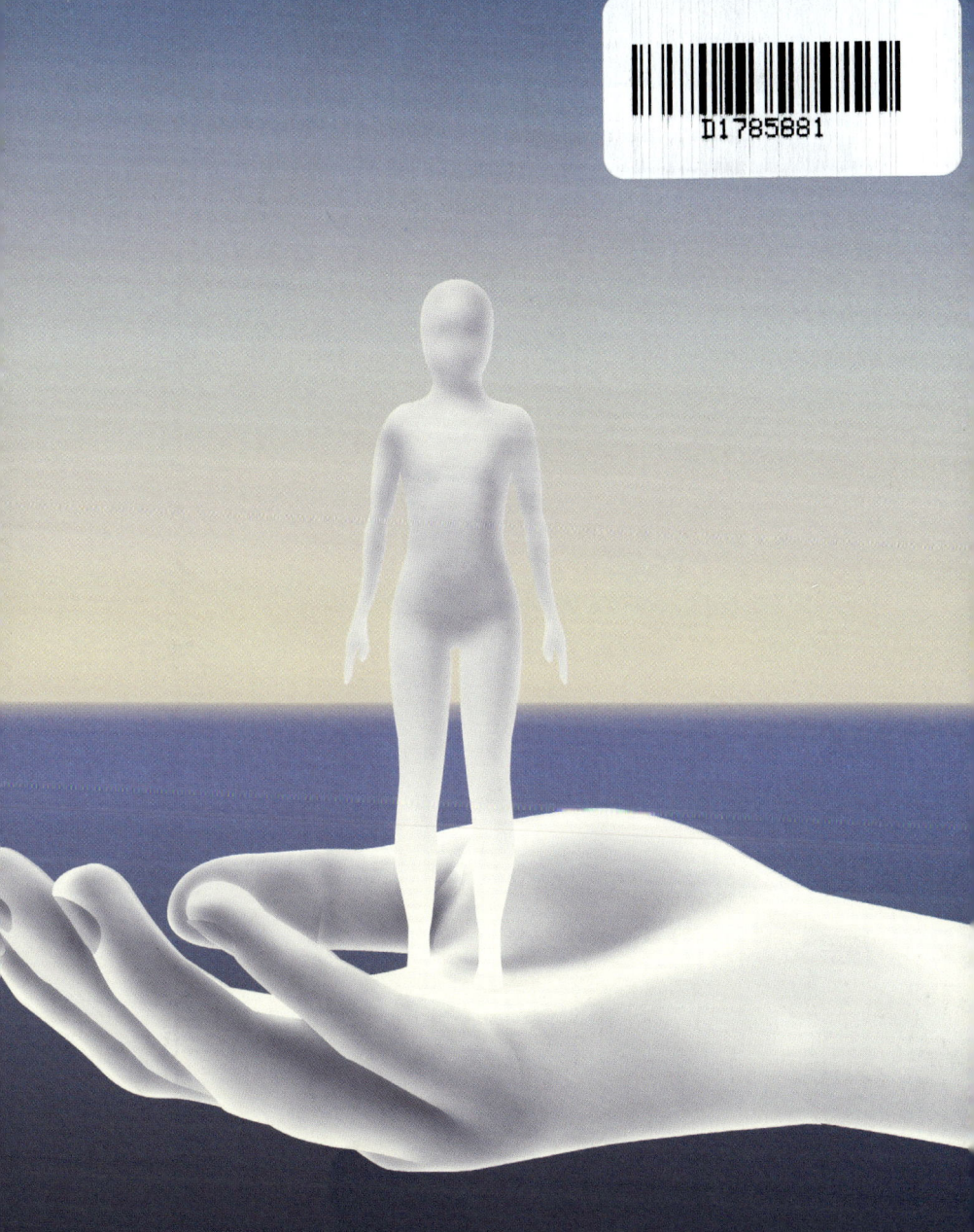

# SOLAR MAXIMUM

FUTUREPOEM BOOKS
NEW YORK CITY
2015

# SOLAR MAXIMUM

SUEYEUN JULIETTE LEE

Copyright © 2015 Sueyeun Juliette Lee

ISBN: 978-0-9960025-2-3

first edition | first printing

This edition first published in paperback by Futurepoem Books
P.O. Box 7687 JAF Station, NY, NY 10116
www.futurepoem.com

Executive Editor: Dan Machlin
Managing Editors: Jennifer Tamayo and Carly Dashiell
Books Editor: Ted Dodson
Guest Editors: Christian Hawkey, Richard Maxwell and Juliana Spahr

Cover design: Everything Studio (www.everythingstudio.com)
Interior design: Nikkita Cohoon (www.nikkita.co)
Typefaces: Franklin (Titles) and Arno Pro (Text)

Printed in the United States of America on acid-free paper

This project is supported in part by the New York State Council on the Arts with the support of Governor Andrew Cuomo and the New York State Legislature. This program is also supported, in part, by public funds from the New York City Department of Cultural Affairs in Partnership with the City Council, as well as by our individual donors and subscribers. Futurepoem Books is the publishing program of Futurepoem, Inc., a New York state-based 501(c)3 non-profit organization dedicated to creating a greater public awareness and appreciation of innovative literature.

Distributed to the trade by Small Press Distribution, Berkeley, California
Toll-free number (U.S. only): 800.869.7553
Bay Area/International: 510.524.1668
orders@spdbooks.org
www.spdbooks.org

*after Stanislaw Lem*

                    for the devastation you opened,
          our awe before it

# CONTENTS

## A PRIMARY MOTHER

THE MEANEST LIGHT DEFENDS YOU
3

IF THERE'S A UNITY IN SENTIMENT
4

AS A MODE OF DAYLIGHT
5

A ROVING BRILLIANCE
6

AN ARRAY BECOMES AN
ORGANIZATIONAL METHOD
7

THE DISTANT SUN IS NOT
SO DISTANT AT ALL
8

WHEN THE TERRAIN IS
A BODY OF WATER
9

A DEVASTATION OF UNKNOWN
MAGNITUDE
11

EVEN THOUGH THE COMPLEX
LANDING WAS ACHIEVED
12

A MANIFOLD BEHAVIOR
13

WHAT ONE WANTS
AND WHAT WILL BE
PRESCRIBED WITHOUT
ONE SINGLE CENTER
FOREVER

15

MENTAL COMMITMENT
ROBOTS

I AM A HAMMERHEAD SHARK.
I MAKE NO SOUND.

33

THE BIG DEAL WITH SHOPPING IS
COMPOSED FOR THE HEART.

44

A DOG IS ONLY ANGRY BECAUSE IT
IS HUNGRY OR AFRAID.

51

WHAT THE HEART LONGS FOR WHEN
IT ONLY KNOWS HEAT.

60

SOLAR MAXIMUM

71

A PRIMARY MOTHER

# THE MEANEST LIGHT DEFENDS YOU

Around the Arctic is an imagined circle, and its resolve depends on our shared imagining. We keep it knit there in a version of stasis with our most basic comprehension: our having to triangulate with harsh extremities from vast distances.

That circle might now be shrinking or vast quantities of it set loose to fail. Sunblindedness is no longer an epiphenomenon, an attendant attitude of danger buried under mounds of quiet. As a roving brilliance, those caught in it truly reckon how the meanest light defends you. Crackling is a great disturbance, but the surface of the sea quietly absorbs even the deepest, most damaging frequencies.

If brightness is a quantity while oceans writhe and heave around it, if the lifeforms that manipulated and characterized the wintry impossible we imagined are true, then we must resolve ourselves to differences, to hazard alongside insight at this—the cold navel of the world.

## IF THERE'S A UNITY IN SENTIMENT

It hasn't been uncovered. To remember something long afterwards without blood ringing in the ears is a small step forwards in the long stream of being. It is beautiful to remember pastels after sunsets, to savor an imagined snowcone when the red lip is all remaining. It is beautiful to love the sound that fails to echo down the hallway when you depress the word for light. If there's a unity in sentiment in language after you dove into the sun, if there's a place on the page to be discovered that can replace body heat or human voices unmarred by space, then it is the most beautiful space, the most beautiful sentence.

Inquiring into replacements for LED lights, of the possible electronic emanations in a freeze, of remaining evanescent without excitement, of broadcasting some haze—these are the semantic blueprints we should build by, the prints in the sand towards various crystal palaces by "sea." The ancient starfish understands this quest, the sea dragon is of a kind. This is the fifth day of February and it is one thousand eighteen degrees outside.

## AS A MODE OF DAYLIGHT

The phenomenon appeared again as a metaphor for dew. The effort exerted to coalesce was found to clear toxins from our blood. We struggle to recognize how these aberrations are in fact larger consistencies in a system we cannot fathom. Such dynamic capacity is at base to us a non-entity, a silence in our understanding we now seek to set aright.

The timetables suggest another minimum, and we turn to the solar system's adrenal storms for any suggestions of a stable core or what our currency might turn into next. Foreign researchers on hand struggle to decipher any synaptic message that would be on par with measurable progress towards an integrated universe. As if silence were ever a simple response. The marginal differences between one magnetic delivery and another require variables of unknowable quantities. The matter is distinctly beside us.

A ROVING BRILLIANCE

An economical manner of saying our animal resilience keeps pace with technology in how our understanding goes hurriedly from here to over there. Determined to overlap with obsolete wires or vatic birdsong, these instruments rely on more than our standing inadvertently on the corner, attentive. Educational ministries mandate how we can alter weather patterns by holding our breath in the bathtub. All of which conforms to suggest that how you make some efforts seem effortless belies the utilitarianism of shine, or keeping pace.

## AN ARRAY BECOMES AN ORGANIZATIONAL METHOD

That we circulate becomes elemental profusion, which we indicate meticulously along a 3-dimensional grid. I move, enamored with a haphazard sense of longing. We dismantle gently. It is a profoundly necessary task.

It grows more difficult to track the space between a transmission and its objects, many of which we capture only via rotation, like a suggested threat. This is filmed—a durational container. The sequence captures both what we are seeing and have ever seen, but backwards into a non-periodized span. A gradual violence takes shape, here in the space we renamed twilight. Its halo hangs over the single ocean, radius a triumphant index of all the walls we've left to climb.

The study proves inconclusive. Our samples suggest a recurring discrepancy, meaning we have to trick the light.

## THE DISTANT SUN IS NOT SO DISTANT AT ALL

It may be more interesting from our point of view to observe the enigma as it appears in fully developed stop-motion photography. How does light arrive? Those fleeting satellites overhead are no matter, the last trails the garter snake left in the grass portend only the patient gap between blindness or solitude (alert to whose suffering). Being alive has again made something new, something that may not be true of justice but is a basic commonplace in evolutionary theory. To forebear is one attitude, rising in an infinite return another.

## WHEN THE TERRAIN IS A BODY OF WATER

This romanticism is a voracious shape between all things in motion, reminding us to stare upwards into the negative space that once housed the brightest phrase. From such a vantage point, the earth's axis intermittently debuts across uneven shores. It reminds us to hurry, to make way across the sliding plateaus whose multi-cresting cascade of waves signal the onslaught of an unknown delivery.

Tell me again: how is it that summer stands now for the place where the body becomes a reservoir, a still placid, a home. That yours was so distantly and fragile, too. And how I ached to move towards.

*the place inside, bright thing star*
*a common citizen in such tense array*
*        insight—the things we read that aren't*
*        addressed to us at all*

A DEVASTATION OF UNKNOWN
MAGNITUDE

To the small star inside, we set up a makeshift rotation that gives us each a momentary relief. Watching is a rudimentary course of action, and we detail each thought as it appears. This is a gentle activity, despite the aggressiveness of the surround. A thought is the beginning of an opening, and we work diligently to trace its aperture, the outline of its extent. When he tells us he simply doesn't know and is unable to track any origins, we recognize the rotation has failed. The small star inside is an obvious integer, but to this he has become blind.

Our job is simple but can lead to a devastation of unknown magnitude. The inconclusiveness of feelings that arise moves with a heat and dynamism analogous to the surface of the sun. In the end, our documents amount to the need for a primary mother. One member of our party becomes obsolete.

## EVEN THOUGH THE COMPLEX LANDING WAS ACHIEVED

Ultimately, those scarlet engines of speculation penetrating this contact lead us into more vigorous wilds. Veridical obstructions refract insight into starlings, plover, a swath of pomegranate seeds scattered on the snow. Now populating an amorous distance, we find it impossible to speak or shape any sounds like the absent moon overhead. The rover addresses itself to a storm. And we, too, stand affixed before that maw.

We give in to a generous blindness that rises like decanted myrrh, a holy perfume. A childish pleasure emerges from this unlikely abeyance. The "sun" spins indeterminately before our dazzled gaze.

## A MANIFOLD BEHAVIOR

From the stereoscope, we categorize alternative kinetic potentials. These indices take on their own volitional energy and move silently—eagerly—across the unfinished floor. Lost scent of magnolias permeates as we navigate through the negative blades.

What happened in the future was graphic. It stands now without a traceable semblance, rather emotional in the way that we've come to trust anger's initial version of events, the posture assumed in a cry. The great task remains: Can we distill the future down to its sheerly psychological components, balancing unresponsive spaces with filled ones—an infinite duration of active listening. Sky.

WHAT ONE WANTS
AND WHAT WILL BE
PRESCRIBED WITHOUT
ONE SINGLE CENTER
FOREVER

*That with music loud and long*
*I would build that dome in air,*
*That sunny dome! those caves of ice!*
*And all who heard should see them there,*
*And all should cry, Beware! Beware!*

—Samuel Taylor Coleridge, "Kubla Khan"

The space of desire,
a destiny modulation

        like a pinprick
        appleblossom on a breeze

enforces a predilection for
what declines or is on the wane

                      *((last aboriginal blooms of the sun-kissed kashmir*

## WELCOME TO MMORPGWORLD

The outside and in
now submerged into a *tectonic* relation—
what is seen and not, transmitted
or held closely in private, a dream

                         *((where contraries and contradictions are disregarded*

I can pay you to observe me in my throes

Enter the SENSORAMA, powered by
FutureYuan, trade commodity of virtuality in stereoscopic 3D!

      "technology is so tethered to our lives
            that it can leave a more specific and
        lasting imprint of a human life
              than history has ever allowed before"

the naked city
    a   constant  "new  babylon"

        echo
        gateway

        dither
        antiquity

        zener waves

Qiu Chengwei stabbed Zhu Caoyuan in the chest
when he found out he had sold his virtual sword

<7,200 Yuan (£473)>

Memories from his detention at Jixi
re-education-through-labour camp in
Heilongjiang province still haunt Liu.
As well as backbreaking mining toil,
he carved chopsticks, toothpicks out of
planks of wood
assembled car seat covers
memorized communist literature to
pay off his debt to society.
By night, he was forced to slay demons,
battle goblins and cast spells

"we kept playing until we could barely see things"

The scarcity of the virtual resource of time,
when novelty stands for a value—
to refute, tally the things gathered
to preclude their circulation

        paper flowers and their folds
        memory of the wind whipping over the sea
        a prisoner's garment
        noblesse of the rehabilitated mind

gulag as a space for disciplined productivity

And the terms for the ordeal,
like speakeasies in the despotic corners of the
trigram omniverse—they unfold as
a negated banality in narration and its designs.
So many syntactic structures blown away by
continuously transforming global currencies—
    from won, to bento, to dragoon to coral smear


*((nearly £1.2bn of make-believe*

roman à clef

        a sense of absence
        riven into time

        prescient liminality      love

        the weight of fiber-optic silk
        syncs our speech

Why is there such enmity between strangers?

The desert. Now it magnifies.

        heat as bondage
                stark quality     night

                blind moon


            (blight a towering hesitation the earth that is
            (toward the ache, slip of fingerbone left there

"The system accurately seizes on the weaknesses of human nature as it calls on gamers to give free reign to depravity in a virtual world that violates the norms of the real world. It gives to those that wage war the power of indiscriminate killing, and it bestows on killers the rewards of increased experience. And the system makes note of your decapitation record. That series of numbers is the height of glory, like an Indian warrior's string of scalps, while all that the dead gain is disgrace."

        incomplete hand prints
        cut frames    the well

                these    our   source codes
                mull over the
                translation ruins

*You don't have any security. Maybe you should take an escort.*

The "pastoral region" once straddling the borderlands of the dissolved nations of Kenya, Uganda, Sudan, Ethiopia, and Somalia finally succumbed to the destructive cycles of flash flood and drought. Where countless generations had depended upon shepherding as the primary means for support, cattle no longer serve as the means to attain security, wealth, or power. As conditions worsened, the cattle raids grew more frequent and fierce—even as the number of cattle in the region diminished. In time, cattle were no longer a consideration: Young men began to raid for glory, honor, and—most importantly—revenge.

\*\*\* may be PrimeDot's most successful launch yet. The company seems to have completely rethought its strategy on how \*\*\* should look and feel, and the results are nothing if not striking. Instead of hewing to the curved, bezeled look, the company has turned the casing and face of \*\*\* into something decidedly more detailed and sophisticated. The materials feel good—premium—in your hands.

> *what is the mechanism of "free trade" by which*
> *a person is allowed to have a certain individuality*

                              the mesh, loose
                              render a people
                              out of desire

                              an experiment of the self:

Though she has invested tens of
thousands of yuan in the game,
she has suffered defeat after defeat
due to the fact that others are
more willing to spend, and
to spend much more money than she.

                    shall i be savage when the banks
                crumble in the dust of this world


  made extravagance & strong




((*The system loves war*

                 museums of glass cases
     covered

bicameral tension
coin silver/purple under eyelids
boil there
cum lit a gamma-ray pop in 'em

vox memo records a blank slide
projected face down huffing sand
        out sides of my mouth

# MENTAL COMMITMENT ROBOTS

*Unlike industrial robots, "Mental Commitment Robots" are developed to interact with human beings and to make them feel emotional attachment to the robots. Rather than using objective measures, these robots trigger subjective evaluations, evoking psychological impressions such as "cuteness" and comfort. Mental Commitment Robots are designed to provide 3 types of effects: psychological, such as relaxation and motivation, physiological, such as improvement and vital signs, and social affects, effects such as instigating communication among inpatients and caregivers.*

—National Institute of Advanced Industrial Science and Technology, PARO

I AM A HAMMERHEAD SHARK
I MAKE NO SOUND

An alternative to an agreement is squeeze, applying acupressure to cartilaginous joints that give under semantic duress. Pursue me across numerous divides, over chasms of understatement now clothed in a subtextual, "common sense" racination. First I am blue and then a movement, a future in song remanded to the stomach, a pair of milky eyes that refuse to triangulate, a stereoscopic ocean floor.

| sounds of water | image of shark in sea |

Transpose this into a watercolor painting, the new scale made possible from sleekly moving across a sandy floor. Sharkness describes a silent skepticism, a roving appetite that sniffs out alterations in the temperature deep beneath a variable surface. To monitor the pH of this environment, all we need do is slit open the skin (the weight of the universe pressing up against an insoluble suit). The range of our telepathic correspondences spans continental rifts, despite their uneven and jagged breaks. A one-to-one correlation is immensely possible, the negative horizon detailing how a reflection is a true opposite, an absented span of the places you inhabited even momentarily. Shark = appetite = roving = blue squeeze.

When the shark burns because the sky is on fire and the ocean is that fire's reflection, there are squadrons of atomic outbursts that also rove the sea, old iron held together by the forces that keep us from knowing and from inside. The world is an iron nut, and the sharks moving through those spaces—both actual and asleep, both breathing and following suit—are always on the verge of a great din. Quietly, they regulate a small manger inside the glowing horizon—how it speaks up when not spoken to, addresses itself merely to the now clamoring past, catching a burning reflection's glow. And on the bottom is without any reluctance, of course, without hesitation because it lacks dew and dew's tears.

*As a shark, I am only about the difference. As an engine made of sharks I do not pose questions. Know only that a shark is hungry and its hunger is eternal, that there is a nowhere inside and that the world is enough for lesser appetites, that the sky is on fire and I am on fire but blue and that blue skin burns without smoke. Distance is a relative distance, always. This way bends when that gun is fired, this wave transfixes that bed of nails, the ones you dropped with yesterday's hands. There is no daylight in the din, shark eyes are infinite eyes. An endless shallow gray smoke that breathes and looks without looking when you swim past.*

| sounds of water | video of shark gill in real time |
|---|---|

Underwater sharks make stop motion resemble perfect symmetry, forecast summer into the lumps behind the gauzy pale between. I don't acknowledge "sky" or "destiny." The underwater shark is blue from the inside and has a blue tongue, a sharp, wedged thing that rasps against the floor we tread so carefully across with bare toes. The shark that reaps our hazards for us, the one that points to each individual cataclysm on the way out, a meandering river of aloe buried under sand. Drink this. Eat that. Follow that. Blue burn, burn. Sharkness *is* destiny, *is* a *perfect* repetition, the imitation that broke through. The very shape of this *perfect* fit, this strident room and arched tunnel—oh forget that you were ever alive and feared death, that there was an outside to your skin and the form you took.

(Tremor of never seeking outs, of following the horizon's nadir

An antique shark is an old appetite and a very old way of knowing. Older is not streamlined, nor is it a primitive condition. It is simultaneous with the hunger and knowledge at work continuously in the sea today. Dark silver, dark light. Soft hermetic transfer I want to press into. Old sound dictates the beat inside, the sluggish sandy drive that occasions this going. Prior to phosphor and before black sands, before the tide became a give and take, the antique shark had its way of meandering, but all directions at that time were one. And they moved into the bluest sun.

An antique shark is a different type of burnish, a warm freeze distilled down into a lithe, resilient body. An antique shark might see things in radio waves or transmit desires via electrostatic currents we register as a minor charge across our skin, the taste of iron against our teeth. I want to capture this resilience. I want to make up the music inside the chord of knowing, the body seeped into and fled. How many coronas have to erupt into glass before we get to collect a residue?

| a shark and its shadow on the sandy ocean floor | a pile of sandy debris |

There are no shark fossils because they are made of cartilage and not bone. The size of your jaw indicates an infinitely wide-awake possibility, and your teeth are many. Because the shark is a muscle and hungry, it works solely in a world composed of its own intuitive making. Shaped a blue space, a blue skin, a blue organ, the shark lacks a heart while occupying its function and form. The outline of a shark on the sea floor retains its animal alacrity, the density of it confounds the way we have come to understand negation and inarticulate necessity. A space is so much more than what precedes or proceeded from it, and the shark is no delay, never out of time, wholly synonymous with verging (a race). But as an ocean's wintry verdancy, a supreme stalk and start, a nothing now of you and elsewhere always, the shark, whether ancient or newly formed, remains.

To resuscitate a shark, to slide two fingers across a serrated organ for "breath," is to wake up inside a starkly blue-lit room where the text written across torn cotton pages wafts in a circular fan's efforts. "This is not a page." "Only you are here." "You are only here." As a shark, are my eyes now made of jet, is this a sonic discourse that we carry on in tides inside our skin, is the way I slide across the page a manner of approaching you at last or scoping out a possible meal. Wake up inside a soluble skin, dissolving into the atmosphere, a nation's rhetorical rain.

## THE BIG DEAL WITH SHOPPING IS COMPOSED FOR THE HEART

The economy is a robotic circulation of love, meaning the Constitution of the United States of America. What you parcel out for yourself remains solely yours but also shared in the most abstracted sense. "Freedom" is a currency and commonplace, given and taken with the same chaste wetness of an open kiss.

I believe you and everything you ever said to me.
Let me pay for this package of Kleenex ($1.49).

| flickering fluorescent bulb | shopping cart rolling slowly down an aisle |

Artificial sunlight lets us see the frailties in the packaging more clearly than we would have otherwise. As a white light, as a striking from a distance and alighting—COMMUNITY—I see all things when I only see you.

*You will buy that which you did not have. That love can be a many-tentacled thing, but maintains a relational resonance suggests a tectonic circuitry. The shadows of two figures hold hands in a terraced mall. The imaginary in this instance is a ray of (artificial) light. Our unconsciousness has built it, a shibboleth cut from snow.*

Dubai is outside the grid but can know the echo of a heartbeat in San Francisco. These train tickets reflect arterial passages through a pulmonary core. If Amtrak boosts the immune system, and United negates neuralgia, the world's capillaries transform into the snowcones we ate in New Orleans after we lay sweating in a bed.

American Heritage Dictionary ($5.99 used).

| superglossy catalog cover featuring an Ikea armchair in red | "you will always be surrounded by true friends" —fortune cookie |
|---|---|

the end of daylight
    forgivable


        (how are we to make this last

Furniture > Spend $125, save 15% **plus** free shipping on select

Baby Gear > Spend $50, get free shipping on parent helpers

Weekly Ad > Electronics deals you've been dreaming of

Furniture
Home
Bed + Bath
Kitchen
Home Decor
Women
Men
Baby

Sports
Toys
Electronics
Movies
Music

## A DOG IS ONLY ANGRY BECAUSE IT IS HUNGRY OR AFRAID

As a child, I had several dogs. Blackie, a fierce mountain forest of deep ravines and the wet creeks that bled through them. Blackie, with dazzling starfruit teeth. Blackie, the face inside the face that I would peek at through the shutters, that I would crawl to through the underbrush, alert to your alertness. There is a forest in the desert where you and I convene. We can drink from a secret spring there, eat from gleaming bowls there, sleep beneath a deep loam that softly falls in over our heads, impenetrable to the sun's glare, a cocoon of damp night in the broadest exposure.

Oh the dogs of war, of God's vengeance, of the hybrid possibilities following a nuclear fallout. Man-made, previously sworn into our allegiance after strict trials, loyalty oaths, performances of stamina, strength, and determination. A submarine dog, a stratospheric dog, an interstellar dog, a hypostatic dog made only of hindquarters and teeth. Are these now our companions and our nighttime guards? The health squads make ready use of them, but a use also tinged with fear.

*Don't be afraid to sleep, the sleep that takes its seconds slowly, that sips them as though through a monarch's curled tongue. This sleep can continue for years, it nourishes your sick neuron receptors, it keeps your saline levels from the breaking point. Continue, push through, continue.*

Tell me it is alright, that I will wake up from this abandonment, that the stranger's hands at work on me are a searchlight across snow. These sutures are friends in disguise, make us communicate with ourselves aided by a new diction. To speak the body is to hold it together. My hand twitches against the bleached paper sheet.

There were dogs that ran outside and in. I would run, too, in a dappled shade. The Potomac River was a place for hiding and running, playing and slipping. Those ferns that grew along those trails, those ferns that curled and softly splayed. How convenient to love their soft, regular lattice work, the interplay of their fronds with the air. I can tell the future in the sunrise and the colors of this stream. West emerged as a colorless conclusion, then, an event horizon after which the highway takes over, hair-like data-strips that dissolve across the tongue. The prints in the ground I track for hours lead me to the place I was taught to call home.

"Tell me, where did you grow up?"
"I also love fresh air and sunshine."

This new treatment, this form of communication, streamlined into a high frequency, pulsar radiation, predicts and precludes all instances of discomfort with a subtlety impossible to the human hand. The need to messily invigorate old synapses with those clumsy probes is now a thing of the past. Patients leave refreshed, rejuvenated, and ready to contribute meaningfully again to our society or exit it with grace. Instances of hypertension and muscular strain declined by upwards of 30%. Though the costs seem formidable now, we are certain that the gains, which have yet to be fully recorded or realized, far outstrip the costs.

A feeling is like the natural production of rain, I remind myself. There are causes that result in the downpour, and to trace them is to understand, to take hold of one's autonomy and ability to decide appropriately one's reactions. There are cycles and rhythms as well, and often a good night's rest can dispel the sudden force with which such things appear. *I must push through to continue.*

This particular feeling is so strictly disembodied that pinpointing its initial causes is hard. A cavalcade of desires—like a bright light behind my eye—threatens to sweep away my sense of stasis. The pull is strong, towards something, but no object sensation in sight. Go, go, go, these feelings say, but not where or towards what. Outside, a dog barks aggressively.

The drama detailed the rise and fall of a merchant family. The young daughter struggles to assert her sense of her unique destiny while her father wrestles with trans-Pacific conglomerates working to keep his tankers from coming ashore. Her break with her family is simultaneous with an off-shore explosion that jettisons hundreds of millions of dollars worth of robotics into the sea. Submarine dogs converge in a hungry swarm. A baby is born in a dark, damp room meant to simulate a forest.

This room inside is better than any other. This forest in the desert, this static place between high frequencies, what hangs on in between amplitudinal shifts and drops. Can I nestle beside you in this darkness hidden from the glaring sun? This room without walls magnifies our sounds, broadcasts your breath back to me, the alertness I am now alerted to. This is a safe space for old dogs, for young boys digging in the earth, for runaway mothers, for the sort of destiny that transmits across bodies and oceans, bypasses circuits in favor of atmospheres and blood.

*I, too, remember a black dog chained to a tree. A mountainous dog of midnight that swallowed the distant sky in a single gulp. Tell me about midnight, about the old song without a melody. There are caverns pocketing distances, there are mirages embedded along the horizon. There are so many distractions to keep us from the center of the hour, so many ways to keep the future from making an appearance. When you cut into the blood, when the chain breaks across the muffled throat, isn't that a new song? Isn't that something to sing?*

## WHAT THE HEART LONGS FOR WHEN IT ONLY KNOWS HEAT

The news from Shenyang, now fallen into the sea, writhes in lasers across evenly distributed stratus clouds. The Dow is up seventeen hundred points. Contemporaneity invites us along, and as a dweller of this partitioned atmosphere, I cannot resist. As for our infinite summer, the endless variety of sauces and nibbling sticks, the badminton we pretend to play as though on command—it is careless of our resistance, our various stands. I feel heavy in the center of my body at this thought. You tell me to mime synchronizing my breath like a mythical combustion engine for fifteen days in response.

Our gains help me remember the second symbol of my name. It varies according to the direction I face or travel in. As a method for triangulation, of finding consonance in the midst of a harmonic gale, it allows me to proceed intelligibly as though marking a stony path traced in winding desert sands.

We park parallel to each other on the concourse, directing the new trans-Pacific hub to rest on a porcelain tarmac. A mental note lodges in my spine—to recount my dreams, in red, to you across a lake filled with snow.

The hub's recoil requires us to desert our posts. And from them we flee.

What is it to be made of water and light, to run towards an end without demarcation? My body resists running, floats along an intelligent track inadvertently attuned to the world market's ups and downs. If this century is best characterized by its heat and speed, we long to be cold, mimicking a damp furnace for night without a sense of hazard in the park.

I spend the day packing "kites" with "snow."

We wander outside the Common Cultures at dusk. Multiple remnants of discarded bodies litter the ground, many manufactured to resemble a lost dream. I move lightly between them, or rather through, and my shadow spells them back together into a continuous statement on individuality and electronics. Captured in a cloudy iris, the sky's reflection no longer seems aberrant. I lean on you, turning in my heart how to unify the light paths you cast against me after hours. A radial semaphore in the distance merges with the tectonic rigs across the horizon. The sight of it calls a short prayer forth from my mouth: a pictograph I dreamed.

We spend the afternoon together watching a docudrama about wild horses that roamed the ancient Arctic Circle. Surprisingly sleek, built for speed and not the weather, they were remarkable for their recklessness. They careen headlong down ice bluffs to fall into a broken heap. We can hear the small, tinny sounds of their terror as they plunge across vast, glowing glacial faces. All of this takes place alongside an abstractly relentless gunmetal sea. I can feel you turn to me, wetness marking the corners of your lips and eyes. I, too, am mesmerized, my vision limited to a sense of motion on the peripheries. Later, I am summoned for an impromptu scan and, miraculously, I pass.

It isn't what you asked for, but with it you make do. There's nothing to hide, you nod to me, because we share it inside our eyes. When we break contact, the data stream zips loose elegantly in a recycled wind. I feel a heavy gas rise within me at the sight, the way those small keys we fingered gently dissolve into mist. I remind myself to be incautious, to make myself as transparent as I can. We are porous, we understand, we are taken up and studied by no entity. Later, I volunteer to mime vacuuming the stairs.

I want to say that you address me from another age, or I live in the future that you dreamed. We wandered here together after I was tossed into a rose-colored storm. The flickering sheets of antiquity brushing across my mind are a hazardous affair, and inside of them I became monstrous and long. The plastered room with one window facing the careless street is overrun with brilliant horses, they came from the other side of the moon and live now on a lake of ice. They run across my memories: I focus very strongly on this and the moment magnifies. The mail arrives to snap me from this reverie. I try hard to return, remain resolute in my emptiness.

We spend a lot of our time together on the new practice of miming collective breathing. I see how this takes us towards another manner of gathering, of setting things aside that are filled with activity and then transformed. Brightness. I am certain this is what powers the recollections we continually strive to have.

We watch them disintegrate in a sidereal gale. As the primary wind rises to its glimmering siren pitch, our gaze breaks. The tarmac requires our adolescence.

After gathering rosemary from the Common Cultures, we sit in a shallow depression and act out sewing them into quilts and handspun cotton clothes. It's too hot, I think, and play dead. It's not the first time I find myself thinking that I'd rather hide behind a cape and rod, or speak through tightly pursed lips to a confused throng. At four, I get up. I've been laying on the sidewalk for three years. Minor stars glimmer dimly across the wall—a gentle reminder that the recycling needs to be taken in, my heart rate entered into the plaque by the mail slot, that it's my turn to climb down into the virtual well. You confront me before I've made up my mind to move, and though it hurts to evaporate in the same way that daylight also suffers, I am satisfied.

At daybreak, then the sun at noon, and later at dusk, memory ever announces the roundness of the era. If I could bloom a begonia blossom or send quills from my thoughts, the gorgeousness of the surround might better mirror the marshaled affect of my dystrophies. Sunlight as glass, or the way our youth is now a token—of what hazy scenes. You assure me that with time and a more strongly developed intuitive connectivity, these things will wash away as *sunlight* changes now into *day*. But most profoundly, I wandered back to this severe instant to find myself already contemplatively crouched in conjecture, aloof and lost in the jet stream's billowing winds.

: SOLAR MAXIMUM

My skin crawls at odd hours of the day, a residual effect of my recent radiation therapies, how they inadvertently synced me to coronal flares. During my morning tea, at the gym, during the drive back home. A simple turn transforms into an avalanching pinprick of tremors one millimeter thick. I'd have preferred a suppurative response—one that collects under the skin—to this invisible, blistering, cracklesome lightning scar. One can't choose the mood that gathers, the body's response.

The brightest moments of the day rarely correlate to a discharge. Gray sky or blackness, a foggy haze aswirl between stars and nothing halts. Some moments tear my teeth.

The news feed portends rolling blackouts across the state. I read over the last of my messages: A blanket request for a plasma donation, Sasha asking if I want a ride to the wake.

---0---

-------

-------

-------

-------

-------

---\---

    frozen impossible, to drag
        a slow and slowing

stop.
        body = filament,
        body = wick, halted.


        body --->
      a bromide to    mind

captured

    held thick, etc.

tremendously—arranged and cast
    (( *informal structures*


        *the bluest dream I dreamt in dark cold*
    *recessed spaces blue*

---

        3 a.m. local time
    according to the USGS


        "These kinds of aftershocks are
    likely to occur for some time"


researchers are baffled by the phenomenon
    there seems to be no clear evidence


    which explains why the
        population of bumble bees

---

I look out the window, wondering that the sky can loom so near. The clouds billow over one another cannibalistically. Heavy like anger, a summer sky about to rain.

Vaguely reflected in the window: Numerous figures mingle about offering condolences, filling plates. A projector casts images against the wall. At the ice-skating rink. Frowning over some books. Her hair whipping in feathers across her face at the shore. Contemplative, laughing, smiling, smiling again. Gently insisting: *in such a manner, remember me.*

*The three-legged crow carries the sun across her back, never detouring from her daily track. She stands on one leg at dawn before she alights, on one leg at noon for her short respite, and lands on one leg at dusk as the hoary sun creeps towards bed past the split ends of the sky. With hollow bones burned black, she quietly carries out this daily task. When she rests, she stretches out her wings, and the entire earth cools beneath her subtle breeze.*

A typical sunspot exists for just a few weeks.
Then it decays, leaving behind a 'corpse' of
weak magnetic fields.
The top of the conveyor
belt skims the surface of the sun,
sweeping up

magnetic fields
old, dead sunspots.
The 'corpses'
are dragged down
at the poles to
a depth of 200,000 km where the sun's
magnetic dynamo can amplify
them.
Once the corpses
are reincarnated (amplified),
they become

buoyant
and float
back to
the surface

((77% of the time the sun was blank
((sun, neither featureless nor steady

She sat up in the hotel bed. I asked her to watch. I put two quarters into my fist. I shook my closed fist as though rolling dice, and when I opened my hand, there were two quarters *and a nickel* nestled in my palm. She was impressed, but I insisted that I could produce much more. I shook my closed hand again. More change appeared in my palm. I kept doing so until coins were falling like rain from my fist. I pressed my two palms against each other as if in prayer, shaking my hands up and down, up and down. Bills started to drop. A few dollars, then a five, a ten, and now several all at once, folded together.

"Keep going!" she yelled, pushing the piling money aside.

*Cold. The blistering of it. A sanitary isolation, this diffusion of kinetic intentions into static, liquid sand. Deeper midnight, negative phosphor darkness. The primary principle requires my concentration, to attend to this liquid summons now, all things gathering to a point, to seep. Heart, liver, lungs, kidneys, all these and more divulge themselves with an igneous notation. And pouring through them, from what else—the dark streams of sunlight's interior. The breaking of, such sorrows.*

        the internal magnetic field    (stressed)
   rises through                   the solar    photosphere,
                                tearing  apart
the uppermost
                            layers of hot plasma

         ((dark patches of sunspot swarms

   violent knots of magnetism
        funnel multi-million degree plasma
from                the inner sun,
             high into the corona

                 (       atmosphere)


            arcades of bright coronal loops

---/---

-------

-------

-------

-------

---0---

My first stereotactic treatment: Initially, I feel fine and am surprisingly unremarkable. After obediently listening to a long monologue, I am allowed on my way. Looking down, I see how from my hands fall phantom slivers of broken glass, leaving a sparkling trail of shards wherever I go.

*You climb up the mountains while surveying the earth, you suspend from the heavens the circle of the lands. Your fierce glare covers us all. Of all the lands of varied speech, you know their plans, you scan their way. You destroy the horns of a scheming villain. You observe, Shamash, prayer, supplication, and benediction, obeisance, kneeling, ritual murmurs, and prostration.*

*Out of mercy you told him where to find the eagle with the cut wings, who would find for him the plant of birth. Out of mercy, you gave us the first law. Out of mercy, speak to me in my dreams, tell me where the deceased lie. You see all things on earth and in hell.*

                        the solar
            magnetic field lines            release a huge amount of
        energy, solar plasma        is accelerated and confined
                within the magnetic        environment (solar plasma
                    superheated particles like protons,
                            electrons and some light elements
such as helium nuclei).                        As the plasma
    particles interact,                    X-rays may be
        generated if the                conditions are right and
            bremsstrahlung
                            is possible.
        (Bremsstrahlung occurs when        charged particles
                    interact, resulting in)
                    This may create

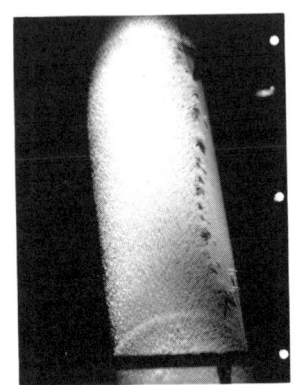

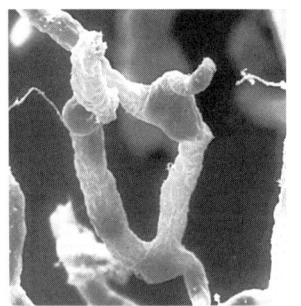

———

 

       with sustained winds during landfall
of 125 mph (110 kts)

 

the third lowest on record
              at landfall (920 mbar)

      "It's too difficult to forecast,"

      thousands of people poured
out of their homes
          and ran

———

((scientists had long suspected that,
((since the molten core is constantly moving,
((changes in its magnetism might be affecting
((surface location of magnetic north

The entire world condenses into a magma skitter *anxious char and crack the* down the throat *hair conductive yank scarlet* across my back down through and toes *choler scorch voracious cling* ———— Seismic fracture blistering, my limbs a shallow raft to quail against—

In the erupting brightness, chest clenched, *she*. Various, multifoliate. Her hands breaking a piece of chocolate to share, chalky flecks peppering her narrow lap, her hands small and shrinking, ever smaller, her face a tiny wisp now on the buzzing, receding horizon.

Sky fades lightly into the soft sounds of dawn. The quakes lessen, reprise themselves now into a meager dirge.

---0---

-------

-------

-------

-------

---\\---

*how did the Sun begin?*

    the fate of a healthy baby does not depend on
    whether it was born naturally

    its progress towards the exterior is painfully slow

*White fires of the body collapsing into another level of insight. Old injuries recede in a tide pulled back, sucked by the gravitational call of a new mode for being. Doubly-helical, entwined, alertness resolves into a murmurous braid. Of all things the starting knew. The pyramidal outflow of offspring from origins, numerously attenuated as a tympan, a sky-blue paradox laminated and caught between the raspy song of those calling from the shore and the distant confabulation of sky, memory, wave.*

*At heart, nestled in the nexus of this chain, the core memory of being born in cold blue, cascading across millennia, translated photochemically to capture the relic of an old word meaning "freeze."*

I kept shaking my hands together, up and down, and now scraps of paper dropped out. Bits of notes I had written over the past year, a small piece of a road map, some waxy receipts. Every time I opened my hands, something new would fall out. She pushed aside the papers building up on the bedspread.

near absolute zero
(about -273°C or -459°F)
reaction rates generally become


molecules are nearly motionless.
life processes     of any organism
cooled near this extreme
should become immeasurably slow,
also any processes of decay.
Actual observation confirms
this theoretical principle.

*(if it is alive, it will remain alive:*
*((if it is somewhat damaged, it will remain somewhat damaged*

Huge coronal loops
can be         seen erupting
from           the solar surface
at solar max,


conditions perfect for solar flares and CMEs

Scattering iridium-plated bones has become the most popular means of divination for telling investors the import of the purchases we make before the next cyclone hits. They relay these quickly between the intermittent bursts in solar static caused by the most recent polarity shift.

I can hardly think straight when the sun roils this way. The most distant satellite composed of a hundred thousand blistering antennae suffering such solar swarms might understand my plight. The shapes heaven allows, conducts into such patterns. And I now a part.

*Exhausted by your daily transformations, the burden of carrying a burning body across the sky, only human sacrifice can regenerate your spirit to rise anew. For the heart houses motion, and you slake after ours. Cut out, in your eagle taloned clutch, we immolate to help speed your way across the horizon again, again, again.*

*Thus we fight, so that time may proceed in its course, the seasons change, the sun feed and return—all to keep the black stellar painting called night at bay. But for all that, eventually you will tire and fail to rise.*

Burr and blur, a dental conundrum now the jaw clattering. Crawling along the bed, sweating, covers askew. Skin a limbus now, other solar patterns on the move I converge on tiled floor, limbs a syncopated half-shelf. Obligatory nodal body. By turns palladium then coal. *Now move.*

a bus


suspended in time


, buried to its

The last time I opened my hands there was a small stack of foreign currency in red. When I leafed through them, they were suddenly contained in a worn, black leather billfold. When I closed the billfold, it became a soft briefcase made of the same black leather. In one of its various exterior pockets, I found some wrapped cigars.

There was a brass clasp on the side, and when I pulled it open I was looking into the floor of a bus. Dewy sunlight cascaded in from the window by the seat. I had an up-close view of the rivets that secured the bus seat to the floor, some litter, a severed hand, its fingers facing me.

How much chemical disorder
can be survived depends on medical technology.
A hundred years ago, cardiac arrest was irreversible.
People were called dead
when their heart stopped beating.
Today death is believed to occur 4
to 6 minutes after the heart stops beating
because after several minutes it is difficult
to resuscitate the brain.
However, with new experimental
treatments, more than 10 minutes of warm cardiac
arrest can now be survived without
brain injury. Future technologies
for molecular repair may extend the

frontiers of resuscitation beyond
60 minutes or more,
making today's beliefs about
when death occurs
obsolete

    merely transitory evidence      a stray boundary between
a much longer-lasting    (*invisible*      opposite polarities
  feature                            the fields annihilate
      the field tries to      one another
        repel the intruder      rapidly


     velocities   directly        shine in emission
     visible                            shortly

       in terms of      before
            brightness             totality

Tell me again your name.
I, too, enjoy fresh air.


*Can we grow otherwise in this immaculate weather, stride forward into a dark blue room indicating the other side of sight? To move towards, push through without continuation. The body quenched into ore—white, august, decipherable ash. Hence.*

*A familiar space. Of a limbic variety. A projected space. Shy dance of hand-drawn soot figures on a screen. A negative space. What longing.*


((black starlight
((consonants

* *If survival of structure means survival of the person;*
* *If cold can preserve essential structure with sufficient fidelity;*
* *If foreseeable technology can repair injuries of the preservation process;*

                      uptempo, the horizon stutters to
        converge

                  SKY

      breath reignites, *heat*
              a constant

          ---/---



                    -------






                                              -------









                              *((when the sun disappears*

NOTES AND ACKNOWLEDGEMENTS

This collection represents my efforts to sketch out a speculative poetics—one that explores the various moods of imagined (future) spaces and their implications for human emotional and psychological being. Despite writing "towards" these imagined futures, my aim is hardly predictive, but reflective. I hope to invite us to meditate more intelligently upon our present—its circumstances, relations, and structures—and envision whether we desire to continue along our current trajectories.

### A PRIMARY MOTHER

An earlier version of this collection appeared as a chapbook published by Least Weasel series of Propolis Press. Brandon Shimoda at the online project "Left Facing Bird" and Patty Payne at *Diode* published earlier versions of individual poems.

### WHAT ONE WANTS AND WHAT WILL BE PRESCRIBED WITHOUT ONE SINGLE CENTER FOREVER

This piece was originally composed as part of a collaborative project on aberrant futures, constructed with Cara Benson, Rachel Levitsky, and Dana Teen Lomax. I am incredibly grateful for the opportunity to have worked with them. It was later published as an e-chapbook at *Drunken Boat*, and I'm especially thankful to the editor, Rebecca Seiferle, for selecting the piece.

A thousand thanks to Nicholas DeBoer for sharing his thoughts and lyric writing about economies; several of the more gestural sections draw from his work.

Other borrowed texts in this piece came from the following sources:

 Vincent, Danny. "China Used Prisoners in Lucrative Internet Gaming Work." *The Guardian* May 25, 2011. <http://www.guardian.co.uk/world/2011/may/25/china-prisoners-internet-gaming-scam>

 Topolsky, Joshua. "iPhone 4 review," *Endgadget* June 22, 2010. <http://www.engadget.com/2010/06/22/iphone-4-review/>

 "Chinese Gamer Sentenced to Life." *BBC News Online* June 8, 1995. <http://news.bbc.co.uk/2/hi/technology/4072704.stm>

 Martinsen, Joel. "Gamble Your Life Away on ZT Online," *Danwei* December 26, 2007. <http://www.danwei.org/electronic_games/gambling_your_life_away_in_zt.php>

 Parenti, Christian. *Tropic of Chaos: Climate Change and the New Geography of Violence.* New York, NY: Nation Books, 2011.

Totilo, Stephen. "In The Virtual World, His Fiancée Never Died." *Kotaku* May 27, 2011. <http://kotaku.com/5806088/in-the-virtual-world-his-fiancee-never-died>

## MENTAL COMMITMENT ROBOTS

An earlier version of the first three poems of this section were published as a chapbook of the same name by Brenda Iijima at Portable Press at Yo-Yo Labs. I'm so grateful for her kind friendship and support.

## SOLAR MAXIMUM

The title poem was written during the beginning of a solar maximum: The sun has its own seasons, which operate on a 22-year cycle. Maximums are noted as periods of intense solar activity (high coronal flares and sunspots). Some scientists conjecture that the earth could be swallowed and destroyed during a solar maximum at some point in the future. Intriguingly, the Mayan calendar dated the end of the world with the conclusion of our most recent solar maximum. Have we survived? Perhaps we continue in the wake of a disaster we hardly marked.

Borrowed texts in this piece came from the following sources:

"Solar Storm Warning." March 10, 2005. science.nasa.gov
O'Neill. Ian. "2012: No Killer Solar Flare." June 21, 2008. universetoday.com

Ettinger, Robert C. W. *Prospect of Immortality*.
Cryonics Institute. cryonicsinstitute.org
Alcor Institute. "What is Cryonics?" Alcor Institute
Life Extension Foundation. alcor.org

Image 1: Nationalmuseum Aleppo, Relief aus Tell Halaf, 14. Jh. v.Ch. Enkidu, Gilgamesch. Ziegler175, December 1987.

Image 2 (Triptych): "The hair-like frost formation has some insulation value on the uninsulated cryo-surface." National Institute of Standards and Technology Digital Collections, Gaithersburg, MD 20899.

"The particles were photographed in exact relation to a 2mm grid spacing." National Institute of Standards and Technology Digital Collections, Gaithersburg, MD 20899.

"A network of capillaries supply brain cells with nutrients. Tight seals in their walls keep blood toxins—and many beneficial drugs—out of the brain." *Bridging the Blood-Brain Barrier: New Methods Improve the Odds of Getting Drugs to the Brain Cells That Need Them.* Ferber D. *PLoS Biology* Vol. 5, No. 6, e169 doi:10.1371/journal.pbio.0050169.

Image 3: "Painting of hands, Foggini-Mesticawi Cave, Gilf Kebir, Western Desert, Egypt" Roland Unger, March 11, 2011.

Special thanks to Jennie Shanker for her photo editing assistance.

This book is set in Franklin (titles) and Arno Pro (text). This first edition, first printing includes 26 limited edition copies lettered a-z and signed by the author.